AI Disclaimer

The information and insights provided herein are generated by an artificial intelligence system designed to analyze trends and data related to high-demand technology stocks. While the AI utilizes advanced algorithms and extensive datasets to inform its conclusions, please be aware of the following: **Not Financial Advice**: The content provided is for informational purposes only and should not be construed as financial, investment, or trading advice. Always conduct your own research and consult with a qualified financial advisor before making investment decisions. **Market Volatility**: The technology sector is characterized by rapid changes and inherent volatility. Past performance is not indicative of future results. Investment in technology stocks carries risks, including potential loss of principal. **AI Limitations**: The AI's insights are based on historical data and patterns, and it may not account for unforeseen events, market shifts, or regulatory changes that could impact stock performance. The AI does not possess the ability to predict future market conditions with certainty. **User Responsibility:** Any investment decisions made based on the AI-generated insights are solely the responsibility of the user. The creators and developers of this AI assume no liability for any financial losses or damages incurred as a result of reliance on this information. **Continuous Learning**: The AI system is continuously updated and trained on new data. Users are encouraged to stay informed and consider multiple sources of information when evaluating investment opportunities. By using this AI-generated content, you acknowledge and accept the above terms and recognize the inherent risks associated with investing in high-demand technology stocks.

Table Of Contents

Chapter 2: The Best Strategy to Purchase the Highest Paying Stocks 2

Chapter 3: Dividend Growth Investing 2

Chapter 4: Value Investing in Undervalued Stocks...........................2
Chapter 5: Growth Stocks with High Potential 2
Chapter 6: Sector-Specific Investment Strategies 2
Chapter 7: Options Trading for Income Generation.........................2
Chapter 8: International Stocks with High Returns........................2
Chapter 9: ESG Investing for Sustainable Profits 2
Chapter 10: Small-Cap Stocks with Big Potential..........................2
Chapter 11: Income-Focused REIT Investments..............................2
Chapter 12: Technology Stocks with High Market Demand 2
Chapter 13: Conclusion and Future Outlook................................2
Chapter 1: Introduction to Tech Investing..1

Chapter 1: Introduction to Tech Investing

The Rise of Technology Stocks

The rise of technology stocks over the past few decades has transformed the investment landscape, creating opportunities and challenges for investors. As the digital age continues to evolve, technology companies have consistently outperformed many traditional sectors. This surge can be attributed to several factors, including rapid innovation, increased reliance on digital solutions, and the expansion of internet connectivity globally. Investors have found themselves drawn to technology stocks, recognizing their potential for substantial returns as these companies redefine industries and consumer behavior.

One of the most compelling aspects of technology stocks is their growth potential. Unlike many traditional sectors, tech companies often experience exponential growth due to their scalability and ability to disrupt existing markets. Investors keen on growth stocks have gravitated toward firms that demonstrate not only strong financial performance but also the capacity for innovation. Companies like cloud service providers, artificial intelligence developers, and cybersecurity firms have emerged as leaders, making them prime candidates for investment. For those employing growth-focused strategies, identifying these high-potential stocks early can lead to significant financial rewards.

Dividend growth investing has also found its niche within technology stocks, albeit in a more selective manner. While many tech companies reinvest profits to fuel further growth, an increasing number are beginning to offer dividends, providing income-focused investors with new opportunities. These firms often prioritize returning value to shareholders through consistent dividend increases, reflecting their financial stability and commitment to long-term growth. Investors looking to blend growth with income can benefit from identifying these dividend-paying technology stocks that show promise for sustained payout increases.

Value investing in undervalued technology stocks presents another strategic avenue for investors. As the market shifts, some tech companies may fall out of favor temporarily, leading to attractive entry points for savvy investors. Conducting thorough due diligence to uncover these undervalued gems requires a keen understanding of market trends and company fundamentals. By focusing on stocks with strong underlying value that the market has overlooked, investors can capitalize on potential rebounds, leading to lucrative returns as the market corrects itself.

Finally, the growing emphasis on ESG (Environmental, Social, and Governance) factors has influenced investor decisions in the technology sector. Companies that prioritize sustainable practices and ethical governance are increasingly favored by investors, particularly as awareness of social responsibility grows. This trend not only aligns with the values of many investors but also positions these companies for long-term success in a world that increasingly values corporate accountability. By integrating ESG considerations into their investment strategies, investors can pursue both financial and ethical returns, ensuring that their portfolios not only perform well but also contribute positively to society.

Understanding Market Dynamics

Understanding market dynamics is crucial for investors aiming to navigate the complex landscape of technology stocks effectively. The technology sector is characterized by rapid innovation, shifting consumer preferences, and evolving regulatory environments. These factors create a volatile yet potentially lucrative investment environment. Recognizing the interplay between these elements allows investors, day traders, and brokers to make informed decisions and capitalize on emerging opportunities while managing risks associated with high-demand technology stocks.

Market dynamics are influenced by various forces, including economic indicators, competitive landscapes, and investor sentiment. Economic indicators such as GDP growth, unemployment rates, and inflation can affect consumer spending, impacting technology companies' revenues and profitability. Additionally, the competitive landscape, shaped by both established tech giants and emerging startups, can create pressures on pricing and market share.

Understanding these dynamics enables investors to identify which companies are likely to thrive and which may struggle in changing conditions.

Investor sentiment also plays a significant role in market dynamics. The technology sector often experiences heightened volatility due to speculative trading and hype surrounding new products or innovations. This can lead to price fluctuations that may not always align with a company's fundamental value. Investors must develop strategies to discern between short-term price movements driven by sentiment and long-term trends based on a company's financial health and growth potential. This understanding is vital for those employing strategies like growth investing or value investing in undervalued stocks.

Sector-specific investment strategies are essential when considering market dynamics. Investors should analyze trends and shifts within the technology sector, such as the rise of artificial intelligence, cloud computing, and cybersecurity, to identify high-potential growth stocks. Additionally, understanding the impact of macroeconomic factors, such as interest rates and international trade policies, can help investors make strategic decisions about which subsectors to focus on. Tailoring investment approaches to these dynamics can enhance the likelihood of securing high-paying stocks and maximizing returns.

Finally, staying informed about global market conditions and regulatory changes is pivotal for successful investing in technology stocks. The rise of ESG investing highlights the increasing importance of sustainability in corporate strategies, leading to a shift in how investors evaluate potential investments. By understanding market dynamics, including the influence of international stocks and small-cap stocks with big potential, investors can build diversified portfolios that align with their financial goals and risk tolerance. This comprehensive approach fosters a deeper understanding of market forces, ultimately allowing investors to navigate the complexities of the technology sector more effectively.

Chapter 2: The Best Strategy to Purchase the Highest Paying Stocks

Identifying High-Yield Stocks

Identifying high-yield stocks requires a strategic approach that takes into account various factors influencing a company's performance and its ability to provide substantial returns to investors. One fundamental aspect to consider is the dividend yield, which is calculated by dividing the annual dividends paid per share by the current share price. Investors should prioritize stocks with a consistent history of dividend payments and increases, as this often indicates financial health and a commitment to returning profits to shareholders. Additionally, examining the payout ratio can provide insights into whether a company can sustain its dividend payments without compromising its growth potential.

In the realm of Dividend Growth Investing, focusing on companies that not only pay dividends but also demonstrate a pattern of increasing those dividends is crucial. Such companies typically have strong cash flow, solid earnings growth, and a competitive edge in their respective sectors. Investors should analyze historical dividend growth rates and assess the company's future prospects, including its market position and industry trends, to forecast its ability to continue this trajectory. Identifying these "Dividend Aristocrats" can lead to a reliable income stream and capital appreciation over time.

Value Investing in Undervalued Stocks also plays a significant role in identifying high-yield opportunities. Investors should look for stocks that are trading below their intrinsic value, often evidenced by low price-to-earnings (P/E) ratios or price-to-book (P/B) ratios compared to industry peers. Conducting thorough fundamental analysis, including examining financial statements, balance sheets, and cash flow statements, allows investors to uncover hidden gems in the market. Companies that possess strong fundamentals but are undervalued present an opportunity for substantial returns, particularly when market conditions improve.

Growth Stocks with High Potential represent another avenue for identifying high-yield investments. While these stocks may not pay dividends initially, they often reinvest profits into expansion and innovation, leading to significant capital gains. Investors should evaluate the company's growth strategy, market demand for its products or services, and competitive landscape. Understanding sector-specific dynamics can help in pinpointing potential high-growth opportunities, particularly in technology, renewable energy, and health sectors, which are poised for rapid advancement.

Incorporating an ESG Investing approach can further enhance the identification of high-yield stocks. Companies that adhere to Environmental, Social, and Governance criteria often attract a growing pool of investors, contributing to stock price appreciation. Furthermore, these companies may benefit from favorable regulatory environments and consumer preferences shifting towards sustainability. Investors should examine ESG ratings and reports, assessing how companies manage their environmental impact and social responsibility. This holistic view not only aligns with ethical investing but can also lead to sustainable profits over the long term.

Timing Your Investments

Timing your investments is a critical aspect of navigating the stock market, particularly in the high-stakes world of technology stocks. Investors often find themselves grappling with the dilemma of when to enter or exit a position. Understanding market cycles, economic indicators, and company-specific developments can significantly influence the timing of your trades. By analyzing macroeconomic trends and sector-specific movements, investors can position themselves to capitalize on opportunities that arise from technological advancements and shifts in consumer demand.

For those engaged in day trading, timing becomes even more crucial. Short-term fluctuations can present lucrative opportunities, but they also come with heightened risks. Successful day traders rely on technical analysis, utilizing charts and price patterns to make informed decisions about entry and exit points. Recognizing the best times to buy or sell can mean the difference between substantial profits and significant losses. Staying attuned to market news, earnings reports, and other catalysts allows traders to react swiftly and effectively.

In contrast, long-term investors may adopt a different approach to timing their investments. Dividend Growth Investing, for example, emphasizes the importance of entering stocks that not only provide income but also have a history of increasing payouts. Timing in this context may involve purchasing shares during market corrections or dips to maximize yield. Value Investing in Undervalued Stocks similarly requires patience and a keen eye for when stocks are mispriced relative to their intrinsic value. By identifying these opportunities, investors can benefit from both capital appreciation and income generation.

Growth Stocks with High Potential represent another area where timing plays a significant role. Investors must evaluate the potential of emerging technologies and how market sentiment shifts can affect stock prices. Investing in these stocks at the right moment, particularly during early adoption phases or just before major product launches, can yield impressive returns. Sector-Specific Investment Strategies also necessitate an understanding of timing, as certain industries may experience cycles of rapid growth followed by corrections, influencing when to invest or divest.

Finally, options trading for income generation and ESG investing for sustainable profits require precise timing to optimize returns. Options traders must navigate volatility and market conditions to ensure they select the right contracts at the right time. Similarly, as environmental, social, and governance considerations gain traction, identifying the right moment to invest in companies that align with these principles can be advantageous. In summary, mastering the art of timing your investments in technology stocks is essential for capitalizing on high-demand opportunities while mitigating risk.

Chapter 3: Dividend Growth Investing

The Importance of Dividends

Dividends play a crucial role in the investment landscape, particularly for those focused on technology stocks within the ever-evolving market. For investors, dividends represent a tangible return on investment that can enhance overall portfolio performance. Unlike capital gains, which are contingent upon stock price fluctuations, dividends provide a steady stream of income. This characteristic makes them particularly attractive in volatile markets, where capital appreciation may not be as reliable. As technology companies mature, many begin to prioritize returning capital to shareholders, making dividends an essential consideration for investors looking for consistent returns.

For dividend growth investing, the focus shifts to companies that not only pay dividends but also have a history of increasing them regularly. This strategy capitalizes on the power of compounding, as reinvested dividends can significantly enhance total returns over time. In the tech sector, several established firms have adopted this approach, signaling financial health and commitment to shareholder value.

Investors who identify these high-quality dividend growth stocks can position themselves for long-term wealth accumulation, benefiting from both regular income and potential capital appreciation.

Value investing in undervalued stocks can also intersect with the pursuit of dividends. Investors often seek companies with solid fundamentals that are trading below their intrinsic value. When these companies offer dividends, it serves as a further validation of their financial stability and potential for recovery. In the tech industry, where innovation can lead to rapid shifts in market positions, finding undervalued stocks that provide dividends can yield significant returns, especially when the market eventually recognizes their true worth.

Growth stocks with high potential are typically not associated with dividends, as these companies often reinvest earnings to fuel expansion. However, a balanced investment strategy may include a mix of growth and income-focused stocks. As some of these growth companies mature, they may begin to initiate dividend payments, providing investors with the best of both worlds. A well-rounded portfolio that includes both growth and dividend-paying stocks can mitigate risks while enhancing overall returns, especially in a sector as dynamic as technology.

Lastly, sector-specific investment strategies can leverage dividends to create income-focused portfolios. For instance, technology stocks that are part of the broader trend toward sustainable and ESG (Environmental, Social, and Governance) investing often attract investors looking for ethical returns. Companies that prioritize sustainability not only appeal to socially conscious investors but may also possess strong fundamentals that enable them to pay dividends. By focusing on these companies, investors can align their financial goals with their values, creating a diversified income stream while supporting the growth of responsible business practices in the technology sector.

Selecting Dividend Growth Stocks

Selecting dividend growth stocks requires a strategic approach that balances potential returns with a keen understanding of the underlying business fundamentals. Investors should begin by identifying companies that not only offer dividend payments but also have a track record of increasing those dividends over time. This characteristic is often indicative of a company's financial health and its ability to generate consistent cash flow. Analyzing the company's earnings growth, payout ratio, and cash flow sufficiency will provide insights into whether a dividend increase is sustainable in the long run.

Investors should focus on sectors that historically demonstrate resilience and growth, particularly within the technology space. Technology companies that prioritize returning value to shareholders through dividends are often those that have achieved significant market penetration and possess a competitive edge. Sectors such as cloud computing, artificial intelligence, and cybersecurity are prime examples where companies not only reinvest in innovation but also reward shareholders with dividend growth, reflecting their stability and profitability.

Another critical aspect of selecting dividend growth stocks is assessing the company's valuation. This involves looking at metrics such as the price-to-earnings (P/E) ratio and the dividend yield. Investors should seek stocks that are undervalued relative to their earnings potential and dividend history. A lower P/E ratio may indicate a stock is undervalued, while a higher dividend yield can signify an attractive return on investment. It is essential, however, to ensure that the dividend yield is not artificially inflated due to a declining stock price, which could signal underlying problems within the company.

Engaging in thorough research and analysis of dividend growth stocks involves monitoring industry trends and economic indicators. Investors should consider macroeconomic factors, such as interest rates and inflation, that could influence a company's ability to maintain its dividend growth. Additionally, keeping an eye on technological advancements and regulatory changes within the industry can provide foresight into potential challenges or opportunities that may impact dividend sustainability.

Finally, diversification remains a fundamental principle in constructing a portfolio of dividend growth stocks. By investing across various industries and geographies, investors can mitigate risks associated with sector-specific downturns. Incorporating both domestic and international stocks, as well as small-cap and large-cap companies, can enhance the potential for stable income while allowing for exposure to high-growth opportunities. This balanced approach is vital for investors seeking to build a robust portfolio that not only generates income but also thrives in the dynamic technology landscape.

Chapter 4: Value Investing in Undervalued Stocks

Recognizing Undervalued Technology Stocks

Recognizing undervalued technology stocks requires a thorough understanding of both the broader market dynamics and the specific metrics that indicate a stock's true value. Investors must look beyond surface-level financials and market trends to identify companies that have strong fundamentals but are trading at a discount. Key indicators include price-to-earnings ratios, price-to-sales ratios, and cash flow metrics. By analyzing these figures in the context of industry benchmarks, investors can spot undervalued tech stocks that may not yet be recognized by the market.

In addition to traditional financial metrics, it is crucial to evaluate the company's growth potential and competitive positioning within its sector. Factors such as market share, product innovation, and management quality can significantly influence a stock's long-term value. Investors should also consider the company's research and development expenditures, as a robust pipeline of new products often indicates future growth. This holistic approach allows investors to distinguish between truly undervalued stocks and those that may appear attractive based on superficial metrics but lack substantive growth prospects.

Another important aspect of recognizing undervalued technology stocks is understanding broader economic and industry trends. For instance, shifts towards artificial intelligence, cloud computing, and cybersecurity can create opportunities for tech companies that are not yet fully capitalizing on these trends. Investors should keep abreast of technological advancements and regulatory changes that may impact the sector. By aligning investment strategies with these macroeconomic trends, investors can better position themselves to identify undervalued stocks that are likely to benefit from emerging market demands.

Investor sentiment and market psychology also play a pivotal role in identifying undervalued stocks. Tech stocks can be subject to extreme volatility due to hype cycles and market speculation. During periods of market correction, fundamentally strong stocks may experience significant price drops, creating potential buying opportunities. Investors should develop a disciplined approach to investing, focusing on long-term value rather than short-term market fluctuations. This mindset can help investors avoid the pitfalls of emotional trading and capitalize on mispriced stocks.

Finally, diversification across different segments of the technology sector can mitigate risks associated with investing in individual stocks. By allocating capital to a mix of large-cap, small-cap, and international tech stocks, investors can enhance their chances of finding undervalued opportunities while managing exposure to sector-specific downturns. Additionally, considering ESG factors can lead to investments in companies that not only demonstrate financial potential but also align with sustainable practices. This comprehensive strategy fosters a well-rounded approach to recognizing and investing in undervalued technology stocks, ultimately paving the way for sustained investment success.

Fundamental Analysis Techniques

Fundamental analysis techniques are essential tools for investors looking to make informed decisions in the rapidly evolving landscape of technology stocks. This analytical approach focuses on evaluating a company's financial health, competitive positioning, and growth potential by examining various factors such as earnings reports, balance sheets, and market conditions. By understanding these underlying elements, investors can better assess a stock's intrinsic value and determine whether it is undervalued or overvalued in the market. This analysis is particularly crucial in the tech sector, where market sentiment can often lead to significant price fluctuations that may not accurately reflect a company's true performance.

One of the key techniques in fundamental analysis is assessing earnings growth. For tech investors, scrutinizing a company's earnings per share (EPS) growth over time can provide insight into its profitability and operational efficiency. Investors should look for consistent EPS growth, which may indicate a solid business model and effective management. This technique is particularly relevant for growth stocks, where high potential returns are often predicated on robust earnings performance. Additionally, examining future earnings projections can help identify companies poised for significant growth, allowing investors to capitalize on emerging trends within the technology sector.

Another critical component of fundamental analysis is the evaluation of a company's financial ratios. Commonly used ratios include the price-to-earnings (P/E) ratio, which helps investors understand how a stock's price compares to its earnings, and the price-to-book (P/B) ratio, which assesses a company's market value relative to its book value. For value investors, these ratios can signal whether a stock is undervalued and present an attractive buying opportunity. In the tech industry, where innovation and rapid change can distort traditional valuation metrics, understanding these ratios is vital for making sound investment decisions.

Cash flow analysis is also a fundamental technique that investors should prioritize. By examining a company's cash flow statement, investors can gauge its ability to generate cash from operations, fund growth initiatives, and return capital to shareholders through dividends or stock buybacks. This is especially important for dividend growth investing, where steady cash flow is essential for sustaining and increasing dividend payments. Companies with strong cash flow can often weather economic downturns better than their peers, making them attractive targets for conservative investors focused on income generation.

Finally, sector-specific investment strategies can enhance the effectiveness of fundamental analysis. By focusing on particular niches within the technology sector, such as cybersecurity, artificial intelligence, or cloud computing, investors can tailor their analysis to better understand industry dynamics and competitive advantages. This approach allows investors to identify high-potential opportunities while mitigating risks associated with broader market volatility. By integrating fundamental analysis techniques with a keen awareness of sector trends, investors can position themselves to make informed decisions that align with their investment goals and risk tolerance, ultimately leading to more successful outcomes in the tech stock market.

Chapter 5: Growth Stocks with High Potential

Characteristics of High-Potential Growth Stocks

High-potential growth stocks are defined by their ability to outperform the broader market, typically characterized by strong revenue and earnings growth. Investors often seek out companies that demonstrate significant market demand for their products or services, often in emerging sectors such as technology. These stocks are frequently found in industries with rapid innovation cycles, where companies can quickly adapt to changing consumer preferences and technological advancements. This dynamism is crucial, as it not only indicates a company's ability to expand but also reflects its capacity to capture and sustain market share amidst competition.

Another hallmark of high-potential growth stocks is their scalability. Companies that can efficiently increase production or expand their service offerings without a corresponding increase in costs are particularly appealing to investors. This scalability often leads to higher profit margins as revenue grows faster than expenses. Investors should look for businesses that have a robust operational framework and the technological infrastructure to support rapid growth. Startups or established firms launching innovative products can exhibit this characteristic, making them attractive targets for those engaged in growth stock investing.

High-potential growth stocks usually exhibit strong management teams with a proven track record of executing growth strategies. Effective leadership is vital in navigating the complexities of growth, from scaling operations to managing investor expectations. Investors should evaluate the backgrounds of executive teams and their experience in successfully scaling businesses in similar markets. A transparent communication style, coupled with a clear vision for future growth, can also enhance investor confidence and lead to sustained stock performance.

Market conditions play a significant role in the performance of high-potential growth stocks. Investors must consider macroeconomic factors, such as interest rates and consumer sentiment, as these can influence stock valuations. For instance, in a low-interest-rate environment, growth stocks typically shine as investors seek higher returns, often favoring growth potential over immediate profitability. Additionally, understanding sector-specific trends—such as advancements in artificial intelligence or renewable energy—can provide insights into which companies may benefit most from increased demand.

Finally, high-potential growth stocks often attract significant investor interest based on their potential for substantial capital appreciation rather than immediate income generation. While some investors may prioritize dividend yields, those focused on growth stocks typically seek price appreciation as their primary return. This focus necessitates a willingness to endure volatility, as these stocks can experience sharp fluctuations based on market sentiment and economic indicators. By identifying the right high-potential growth stocks, investors can position themselves to capitalize on substantial returns while navigating the inherent risks associated with growth investing.

Evaluating Growth Potential

Evaluating the growth potential of technology stocks is a crucial step for investors seeking to capitalize on the fast-paced evolution of the tech industry. Growth potential encompasses various factors, including market trends, company fundamentals, and competitive positioning. Investors must analyze these elements to identify stocks with the highest likelihood of substantial appreciation. This evaluation process should begin with an assessment of a company's market position and its capacity to innovate. Companies that consistently develop cutting-edge products or services often enjoy a competitive edge that can translate into significant market share gains.

Another vital aspect of evaluating growth potential is examining financial metrics such as revenue growth rates, earnings per share (EPS), and profit margins. Investors should look for companies that demonstrate sustained revenue growth, ideally exceeding industry averages. This indicates a robust demand for the company's offerings and suggests the potential for future profitability. Additionally, analyzing EPS trends can provide insight into how effectively a company is managing its costs and enhancing shareholder value. A focus on profit margins can reveal a company's operational efficiency and pricing power within its market niche.

Investors should also consider macroeconomic factors and industry trends that could impact a company's growth trajectory. For instance, the increasing reliance on cloud computing, artificial intelligence, and cybersecurity solutions presents significant opportunities for technology companies operating in these sectors. Understanding these trends enables investors to align their portfolios with sectors poised for expansion. Moreover, evaluating how well a company adapts to changes in technology and consumer preferences is essential, as adaptability is a key determinant of long-term success in the tech landscape.

Another strategy in evaluating growth potential involves analyzing a company's management team and their strategic initiatives. A strong leadership team with a clear vision can drive innovation and effectively navigate market challenges. Investors should investigate past performance, decision-making processes, and the company's strategic direction to gauge the likelihood of future success. Additionally, examining a company's investment in research and development (R&D) can provide insights into its commitment to growth and innovation, as companies that prioritize R&D are often better positioned to seize emerging opportunities.

Lastly, diversification within the tech sector can enhance growth potential while managing risk. Investors should consider a mix of large-cap, mid-cap, and small-cap technology stocks, as each category offers unique growth opportunities. Small-cap stocks, in particular, can provide significant upside potential, although they may also carry higher risk. Moreover, incorporating sector-specific investment strategies and options trading for income generation can further optimize growth potential while balancing the inherent volatility of technology stocks. By thoroughly evaluating these factors, investors can make informed decisions that capitalize on the dynamic nature of the tech industry.

Chapter 6: Sector-Specific Investment Strategies

Technology Sector Overview

The technology sector has emerged as a cornerstone of modern economies, characterized by rapid innovation and significant market growth. From software and hardware to telecommunications and emerging technologies like artificial intelligence and blockchain, the sector encompasses a wide array of industries that collectively shape the global landscape. Investors are increasingly drawn to tech stocks due to their potential for high returns and the integral role these companies play in everyday life. Understanding the dynamics of this sector is essential for any investor looking to capitalize on opportunities that arise from technological advancements.

One of the defining features of the technology sector is its relentless pace of innovation, which drives both growth stocks and value investments. Companies that invest heavily in research and development often outperform their peers, as they can introduce groundbreaking products and services that meet evolving consumer demands. For investors focused on growth stocks, identifying firms that demonstrate strong earnings potential and robust market positioning is crucial. These companies often have high price-to-earnings ratios, reflecting their anticipated growth trajectories. On the other hand, value investors may seek out established technology firms that are undervalued relative to their intrinsic worth, presenting opportunities for significant capital appreciation.

Dividend growth investing has also gained traction within the technology sector, as more companies recognize the importance of returning capital to shareholders. Firms like Microsoft and Apple have transitioned from being solely growth-oriented to also providing consistent dividends, appealing to income-focused investors. This shift allows investors to benefit from both capital appreciation and a steady income stream. For those interested in longer-term strategies, selecting technology stocks with a history of increasing dividends can lead to a lucrative investment strategy, especially in an era where income generation is essential for many portfolios.

Moreover, the rise of environmental, social, and governance (ESG) investing has influenced investment strategies in the technology sector. Investors are increasingly prioritizing companies that demonstrate a commitment to sustainability and ethical practices. This trend has led to the emergence of technology companies that not only focus on profitability but also on creating positive societal impacts. As a result, tech firms that align with ESG principles are often viewed as more stable investments, appealing to a growing demographic of socially conscious investors. This shift not only reflects changing consumer preferences but also signals a broader trend that could reshape the investment landscape.

Lastly, the technology sector offers unique opportunities for options trading and investing in international stocks. Options trading can provide investors with income generation opportunities through strategies such as covered calls or cash-secured puts, particularly in high-demand tech stocks. Additionally, the globalization of technology means that investors can explore markets beyond their borders, identifying international stocks with high returns in emerging economies. This diversification can enhance portfolio resilience while tapping into growth segments that may be overlooked domestically. By understanding these multifaceted aspects of the technology sector, investors can formulate informed strategies to navigate its complexities and maximize their investment potential.

Investment Strategies by Technology Subsector

Investment strategies within the technology subsector can vary significantly based on the specific niche an investor chooses to focus on. For those looking to purchase high-paying stocks, it is essential to analyze companies that not only have robust earnings but also a history of consistent dividend growth. Dividend Growth Investing emphasizes firms that regularly increase their payouts, making them attractive for income-focused investors. Companies like Microsoft and Apple have established records of dividend increases while maintaining strong cash flow, offering a dual advantage of capital appreciation and income generation.

Value Investing in Undervalued Stocks is another approach that resonates well in the tech sector, especially during periods of market correction. Investors should look for firms with solid fundamentals that are trading below their intrinsic value. Often, smaller tech companies or those in niche markets may not receive the attention they deserve, creating opportunities. For instance, companies involved in cybersecurity or cloud computing that are currently undervalued could provide significant upside potential as market awareness grows.

Growth Stocks with High Potential remain a staple for investors willing to take on more risk. These stocks are typically from companies that exhibit rapid earnings growth and can significantly outperform the broader market. Identifying emerging technologies, such as artificial intelligence or quantum computing, can lead to lucrative investments. Firms like Nvidia, which have positioned themselves as leaders in these innovative sectors, often present compelling growth narratives that can attract both institutional and retail investors.

Sector-specific investment strategies are critical for capitalizing on trends within the technology space. For example, focusing on software-as-a-service (SaaS) companies can yield high returns due to their recurring revenue models. Investors can apply a similar approach to emerging subsectors like fintech or health tech, where the demand for innovative solutions continues to surge. By honing in on these specific areas, investors can better align their portfolios with market trends and consumer needs.

Options Trading for Income Generation is a sophisticated strategy that allows investors to enhance returns while managing risk. By selling covered calls on high-demand technology stocks, investors can generate additional income from their existing holdings. Moreover, exploring International Stocks with High Returns can diversify a tech-focused portfolio, exposing investors to growth opportunities in markets like Asia and Europe. Finally, incorporating ESG Investing for Sustainable Profits can attract socially conscious investors who seek to support companies that prioritize environmental, social, and governance factors, further solidifying their investment strategy in today's landscape.

Chapter 7: Options Trading for Income Generation

Basics of Options Trading

Options trading is a versatile investment strategy that allows investors to speculate on the future price movements of underlying assets, such as stocks, without needing to own them outright. At its core, an option is a contract that grants the buyer the right, but not the obligation, to purchase or sell an underlying asset at a predetermined price, known as the strike price, before a specified expiration date. This unique characteristic of options provides flexibility for various investment strategies, including hedging against market volatility and generating income through premium collection.

There are two primary types of options: call options and put options. A call option gives the buyer the right to purchase the underlying asset at the strike price, while a put option gives the buyer the right to sell it. Investors utilize call options when they anticipate an increase in the asset's price, whereas put options are employed when they expect a decline. Understanding the dynamics of these options is essential for investors looking to leverage market movements in technology stocks or other high-demand sectors.

One of the key benefits of options trading is the potential for significant returns with a relatively small initial investment. By purchasing options, investors can control a larger amount of shares than they could by purchasing the stock outright. This leverage can amplify profits when trades go in the investor's favor. However, it is crucial to recognize that this leverage also increases risk, as options can expire worthless if the underlying asset does not move in the anticipated direction, leading to a complete loss of the premium paid.

Incorporating options into a broader investment strategy can enhance income generation. For instance, income-focused investors can utilize covered calls, a strategy where they sell call options against stocks they already own. This allows investors to collect premiums while potentially selling their shares at a higher price if the stock rises above the strike price. Such strategies are particularly attractive in a technology sector characterized by rapid price movements and volatility, providing both income and growth potential.

Options trading is not without its complexities, and investors must educate themselves on the various strategies, risks, and market conditions that impact options pricing. Tools like the options chain, implied volatility, and Greeks—Delta, Gamma, Theta, and Vega—are essential for making informed trading decisions. As technology stocks continue to dominate market interest, a solid understanding of options trading can enhance an investor's ability to navigate this dynamic landscape, whether they are focusing on growth stocks, dividend growth, or sector-specific strategies.

Strategies for Generating Income

Investors looking to capitalize on the rapidly evolving technology sector can adopt various strategies to generate income from their investments. One effective approach is Dividend Growth Investing, where investors focus on stocks that not only pay dividends but also have a track record of increasing those dividends consistently. This strategy is particularly appealing in the tech industry, where certain established companies offer reliable dividend growth due to their strong cash flows and competitive moat. By reinvesting these dividends, investors can compound their returns over time, creating a sustainable income stream.

Value Investing in Undervalued Stocks is another strategy that can yield significant returns. This approach involves identifying technology stocks that are trading below their intrinsic value, often due to market overreactions or temporary setbacks. Investors can analyze financial metrics such as price-to-earnings ratios and cash flow to uncover these hidden gems. When the market eventually recognizes the true value of these stocks, investors can benefit from both appreciation in stock price and potential dividends, thereby generating income over time.

Growth Stocks with High Potential represent a lucrative avenue for income generation, albeit with a different risk profile. These stocks are typically characterized by their strong earnings growth and the ability to reinvest profits back into the business for expansion. While they may not pay dividends initially, the capital appreciation potential can lead to substantial returns. Investors focusing on growth stocks must conduct thorough research to identify companies with innovative products, strong management teams, and market demand that could drive future earnings.

Options Trading for Income Generation offers a more advanced strategy for investors willing to navigate the complexities of the options market. By writing covered calls or selling puts, investors can generate premium income while still holding onto their tech stocks. This strategy can work particularly well in a stable or slightly bullish market, allowing investors to enhance their returns on existing holdings. However, it requires a solid understanding of options mechanics and market conditions to implement effectively.

Finally, exploring International Stocks with High Returns can provide diversification and potential income for investors. Many tech companies outside the U.S. are positioned for growth and may offer attractive dividend yields. By investing in international markets, investors can tap into emerging technological advancements and varying economic cycles. Additionally, ESG Investing for Sustainable Profits is gaining traction, where investors focus on companies with strong environmental, social, and governance practices. This strategy not only aligns with ethical investing principles but can also lead to long-term profitability, as these companies are often better positioned to navigate regulatory changes and shifting consumer preferences.

Chapter 8: International Stocks with High Returns

Opportunities in Global Markets

Opportunities in global markets have become increasingly attractive for investors looking to diversify their portfolios and tap into high-demand technology sectors. The expansion of technology companies across borders has created a landscape filled with potential for growth stocks, particularly those in emerging markets. Investors can benefit from identifying undervalued stocks in these regions, as they often provide opportunities for significant returns. By focusing on global market trends and leveraging local insights, investors can strategically position themselves to take advantage of the next wave of technological innovation.

One promising avenue is the growth of international stocks with high returns. Many tech firms in countries such as India, Southeast Asia, and parts of Africa are experiencing rapid growth driven by increasing internet penetration and mobile device adoption. These markets present a fertile ground for value investing, where investors can find undervalued companies poised for expansion. By conducting thorough research and analysis, investors can uncover hidden gems that may not yet be on the radar of mainstream investors, allowing for a potentially lucrative entry point.

Sector-specific investment strategies also play a crucial role in capitalizing on global market opportunities. Investors should consider sectors such as fintech, e-commerce, and renewable energy, which are gaining traction worldwide. By focusing on these sectors, investors can align their portfolios with long-term trends that promise sustainable growth. Moreover, incorporating ESG (Environmental, Social, and Governance) criteria into investment decisions can enhance returns while also supporting ethical practices, making a case for sustainable profits that appeal to a growing base of socially conscious investors.

Small-cap stocks, often overlooked in favor of larger, more established companies, can offer substantial growth potential in the global arena. These companies, particularly in technology, can scale rapidly, providing investors with high-risk, high-reward investment opportunities. By diligently researching and identifying promising small-cap tech stocks, investors can seize opportunities that larger firms may miss. This strategy requires a keen eye for market dynamics and a willingness to engage in options trading for income generation as a complementary tactic.

Lastly, income-focused investments, such as Real Estate Investment Trusts (REITs), can provide a stable income stream while benefiting from global market growth. These instruments allow investors to participate in the real estate sector's profits, which can be particularly lucrative in rapidly urbanizing regions. Integrating a mix of high-demand technology stocks and income-generating assets creates a balanced investment strategy that effectively mitigates risks while capitalizing on the expansive opportunities present in global markets. By remaining informed and adaptive, investors can navigate the complexities of international investing and harness the potential for significant returns.

Analyzing International Technology Stocks

Analyzing international technology stocks requires a multifaceted approach, considering both macroeconomic factors and specific characteristics of the tech sector. Investors must first examine the economic environment of the countries in which these companies operate. Factors such as GDP growth, inflation rates, and currency fluctuations can significantly impact the performance of international stocks. A robust economy often fosters innovation and investment, leading to higher stock prices, while economic instability can hinder growth and negatively affect returns. Additionally, understanding the regulatory landscape is crucial, as different countries have varying laws regarding technology, data privacy, and intellectual property that can influence a company's operations and profitability.

When evaluating individual technology stocks, investors should focus on key performance metrics such as revenue growth, profit margins, and market share. These indicators can provide insights into a company's operational efficiency and competitive positioning within its sector. Investors should also consider the company's research and development (R&D) spending, as this is a critical driver of innovation in the tech industry. Successful tech companies often reinvest a significant portion of their profits back into R&D to maintain their competitive edge. Evaluating a company's product pipeline and technological advancements can help investors identify growth stocks with high potential for future returns.

Another essential aspect of analyzing international technology stocks is understanding market trends and consumer behavior in different regions. The demand for technology products and services can vary significantly across global markets due to cultural preferences, technological adoption rates, and economic conditions. Investors should pay attention to emerging markets, where rapid urbanization and increasing internet penetration can lead to substantial growth opportunities. Additionally, sector-specific investment strategies can help investors pinpoint which areas within the tech industry are poised for expansion, such as cloud computing, artificial intelligence, or cybersecurity.

Incorporating ESG (Environmental, Social, and Governance) criteria into investment analysis is becoming increasingly important for investors focused on sustainable profits. Companies that prioritize sustainability and ethical practices often enjoy stronger brand loyalty and can mitigate risks associated with regulatory changes. Investors should seek out international tech stocks that not only demonstrate financial performance but also adhere to high ESG standards. This approach not only aligns with the values of socially conscious investors but can also lead to long-term financial success, as companies with strong ESG practices are often better positioned to navigate challenges and capitalize on new opportunities.

Finally, for those interested in options trading and income generation from international technology stocks, understanding the volatility and liquidity of these investments is vital. Options can be a powerful tool for investors seeking to hedge their positions or generate additional income through selling covered calls. However, the unique dynamics of international markets can lead to increased volatility, which can amplify both risks and rewards. Investors should ensure they have a solid grasp of the specific risks associated with trading options in these markets, including geopolitical risks and currency exposure, to develop effective strategies that align with their investment goals.

Chapter 9: ESG Investing for Sustainable Profits

Understanding ESG Criteria

Understanding ESG criteria has become essential for investors seeking to align their portfolios with sustainable and ethical practices. Environmental, Social, and Governance (ESG) criteria provide a framework for evaluating a company's operations and performance in areas that may impact long-term financial returns. Investors who incorporate ESG factors into their decision-making processes often find that these criteria not only reflect a company's commitment to responsible management but also serve as indicators of its future growth potential.

The environmental aspect of ESG pertains to how a company interacts with the natural environment. This includes its carbon footprint, waste management practices, resource conservation, and overall commitment to sustainability. Companies that prioritize environmental stewardship often enjoy competitive advantages, such as reduced energy costs and better regulatory compliance. For investors, identifying firms with strong environmental practices can lead to capitalizing on the growing demand for green technologies and sustainable products.

Social criteria focus on a company's relationships with employees, suppliers, customers, and the communities in which it operates. Factors such as labor practices, human rights, diversity and inclusion, and community engagement are evaluated under this umbrella. A company that excels in social responsibility is likely to foster a positive reputation, attract top talent, and maintain customer loyalty. Investors can benefit from investing in firms that prioritize social initiatives, as these companies often experience lower turnover rates and enhanced brand loyalty, ultimately driving profitability.

Governance involves the company's leadership, executive pay, audits, internal controls, and shareholder rights. Effective governance structures are critical for mitigating risks and ensuring that management acts in the best interests of shareholders. Companies with transparent and accountable governance practices are generally viewed as less risky investments. By focusing on governance, investors can identify firms that are well-positioned to navigate market challenges and regulatory changes, leading to more stable financial performance.

Incorporating ESG criteria into investment strategies aligns with the increasing awareness of sustainable investing among both retail and institutional investors. As the demand for responsible investment options grows, companies that excel in ESG practices are likely to attract more capital, potentially leading to higher stock prices and returns over time. For those involved in sectors such as technology, where innovation and ethical practices are paramount, understanding ESG criteria not only aids in selecting high-potential growth stocks but also fosters a portfolio that contributes positively to society and the environment.

Identifying ESG-Compliant Technology Companies

Identifying ESG-compliant technology companies requires a careful analysis of various factors that contribute to a firm's commitment to environmental, social, and governance principles. Investors should start by evaluating a company's public disclosures, which often include sustainability reports and ESG ratings from reputable agencies. These documents typically outline a firm's initiatives in reducing carbon footprints, promoting diversity, and ensuring ethical governance practices. By scrutinizing these reports, investors can gain insights into a company's operational transparency and accountability, which are critical components of ESG compliance.

In addition to reviewing public disclosures, investors should consider third-party ESG ratings that benchmark companies against their peers. These ratings, provided by organizations like MSCI, Sustainalytics, and Refinitiv, offer a comparative analysis that can simplify the screening process. A high ESG rating indicates a company's strong performance in sustainability and social responsibility, making it a potentially attractive investment. However, investors should be cautious of relying solely on these ratings; a comprehensive evaluation should also include qualitative factors, such as company culture and leadership commitment to ESG goals.

Another vital aspect of identifying ESG-compliant technology companies is to explore their product and service offerings. Companies that prioritize sustainability often develop innovative technologies that address environmental issues, such as renewable energy solutions, energy-efficient products, and sustainable supply chain practices. Investors should look for firms that not only comply with ESG standards but also lead in creating technologies that contribute positively to society and the environment. This alignment of business strategy with ESG principles can enhance long-term growth potential and appeal to a socially conscious investor base.

Engagement with stakeholders is another indicator of a company's ESG commitment. Technology firms that actively engage with their employees, customers, and communities demonstrate a dedication to social responsibility. This can be assessed through initiatives such as employee training programs, community investment, and customer feedback mechanisms. Investors should seek companies that foster inclusive environments and prioritize stakeholder interests, as these practices can lead to enhanced brand loyalty and reputational strength, ultimately benefiting financial performance.

Finally, investors should remain vigilant about regulatory changes and evolving standards associated with ESG compliance. Governments and international organizations are increasingly implementing regulations that require transparency in ESG practices. Keeping abreast of these developments can aid investors in identifying companies that not only meet current standards but are also positioned to thrive in a landscape that increasingly values sustainability. By focusing on these critical elements, investors can effectively identify technology companies that are not only ESG-compliant but also poised for sustainable profitability in the long term.

Chapter 10: Small-Cap Stocks with Big Potential

Advantages of Investing in Small-Cap Stocks

Investing in small-cap stocks presents a unique opportunity for investors seeking substantial growth potential. Small-cap stocks, defined as companies with a market capitalization typically between $300 million and $2 billion, are often overlooked by larger institutional investors. This lack of attention can create an advantageous environment for individual investors who are willing to conduct thorough research and identify promising companies. As these businesses expand, they can offer exponential returns that are less frequently found in larger, established firms.

One of the primary advantages of small-cap stocks is their potential for rapid growth. Many small-cap companies are in the early stages of development, with innovative products or services that cater to emerging markets or unmet consumer needs. Investors who identify these growth opportunities early can benefit significantly as the companies scale operations and increase market share. This makes small-cap stocks particularly appealing for growth-focused investors who are looking for the next big tech titan to emerge.

Another key benefit of investing in small-cap stocks is the potential for undervaluation. These companies often trade at lower price-to-earnings ratios compared to their large-cap counterparts, which can indicate that they are undervalued in the market. Value investors can take advantage of this discrepancy by purchasing shares at a lower price, anticipating that as the market recognizes the company's true worth, the stock price will rise. This strategy aligns well with those focused on finding undervalued stocks that possess strong fundamentals and growth potential.

Small-cap stocks also provide diversification benefits within a broader investment portfolio. Given their different risk and return profiles, they can help balance investments across various sectors and markets. In particular, tech-related small-cap stocks can be an excellent addition for investors focused on sector-specific strategies, as they often operate in high-demand niches such as software development, cybersecurity, and renewable energy technology. This diversification can mitigate risk while enhancing the potential for higher returns, particularly in a rapidly evolving tech landscape.

Lastly, investing in small-cap stocks can lead to greater engagement and research opportunities for investors. Unlike large-cap companies, which are often covered extensively by analysts and the media, small-cap companies may not have the same level of scrutiny. This allows investors to gather insights directly from company communications, industry reports, and financial filings, enabling a more hands-on approach to investing. For those who thrive on research and analysis, small-cap stocks can provide a fulfilling experience as they navigate the nuances of identifying and capitalizing on high-potential investments in the tech industry.

Strategies for Identifying Promising Small-Caps

Identifying promising small-cap stocks requires a strategic approach that combines thorough research, market understanding, and analytical skills. Investors should begin by defining their investment criteria, focusing on key metrics such as revenue growth, earnings potential, and market positioning. Small-cap stocks, typically defined as companies with a market capitalization of $300 million to $2 billion, often represent untapped opportunities in niche markets. By setting specific thresholds for financial performance and growth potential, investors can narrow their search to companies that align with their investment philosophy, whether it be value investing or growth investing.

Another effective strategy involves leveraging financial ratios and metrics to assess the viability of small-cap investments. Key indicators such as price-to-earnings (P/E) ratio, debt-to-equity ratio, and return on equity (ROE) provide insights into a company's financial health and operational efficiency. Investors should also consider the PEG ratio, which factors in earnings growth rates and provides a clearer picture of valuation relative to growth prospects. This quantitative analysis can reveal undervalued stocks or those with strong growth trajectories, essential for making informed investment decisions in a competitive market.

In addition to financial metrics, qualitative factors play a crucial role in identifying promising small-caps. Investors should evaluate the management team, their track record, and strategic vision for the company. A strong, experienced management team can significantly impact the potential for growth and innovation. Furthermore, understanding the industry landscape, including competitive positioning and market trends, can provide context for a company's future performance. Investors should also analyze customer satisfaction and brand loyalty, as these elements can influence long-term success and revenue stability.

Networking and gaining insights from industry experts can further enhance an investor's ability to identify promising small-cap stocks. Engaging with brokers, attending industry conferences, and participating in investment webinars can provide valuable information about emerging trends and innovative companies. These connections often lead to discovering hidden gems that may not yet be on the radar of mainstream investors. Additionally, staying informed about regulatory changes and technological advancements can provide a competitive edge, allowing investors to anticipate shifts that may affect small-cap stocks.

Finally, diversification remains a fundamental strategy for managing risk when investing in small-cap stocks. Given their inherent volatility, a diversified portfolio can cushion against potential losses while still allowing for participation in high-growth opportunities. By spreading investments across different sectors and industries, investors can mitigate the risks associated with individual companies. Whether through direct investment in small-cap stocks, sector-specific funds, or exchange-traded funds (ETFs), diversification helps ensure that investors capitalize on the potential high returns of small-cap investments while managing overall portfolio risk effectively.

Chapter 11: Income-Focused REIT Investments

Understanding Real Estate Investment Trusts

Real Estate Investment Trusts (REITs) have emerged as a compelling avenue for investors seeking income and diversification within their portfolios. These companies own, operate, or finance income-producing real estate across a range of property sectors. By pooling capital from numerous investors, REITs enable individuals to invest in large-scale, income-generating real estate without the need to purchase or manage property directly. This structure not only democratizes access to real estate but also provides a platform for individuals interested in dividend growth investing, as most REITs are required to distribute at least 90% of their taxable income to shareholders in the form of dividends.

Investors looking for high-paying stocks will find that many REITs offer attractive dividend yields, often surpassing those of traditional equities. The income generated from rental properties, coupled with the potential for capital appreciation, positions REITs as a robust option for income-focused investment strategies. This is particularly appealing in a low-interest-rate environment, where traditional fixed-income securities may fall short of meeting income needs.

By incorporating REITs into a broader investment strategy, investors can enhance their cash flow while benefiting from the potential for long-term asset appreciation.

The diversity of REITs allows for sector-specific investment strategies. Different types of REITs focus on various sectors, including residential, commercial, healthcare, and industrial properties. For example, a residential REIT may benefit from trends in urbanization and increased demand for rental housing, while a healthcare REIT could thrive in an aging population that demands more medical facilities. By understanding the nuances of these sectors, investors can strategically allocate their resources to capitalize on growth opportunities and mitigate risks associated with economic fluctuations.

Moreover, REITs can be an attractive option for those interested in ESG investing for sustainable profits. Many REITs are increasingly focused on environmentally responsible practices, energy-efficient buildings, and sustainable development. By investing in REITs that prioritize these values, investors not only align their portfolios with their ethical beliefs but also tap into a growing market that is gaining traction among socially conscious investors. This alignment can lead to enhanced brand loyalty and potentially lower operational costs, contributing to overall profitability.

Finally, for those intrigued by small-cap stocks with big potential, certain niche REITs may offer the opportunity for substantial returns. While larger, well-established REITs can provide stability and consistent dividends, smaller or emerging REITs may present higher growth potential, albeit with increased risk. By conducting thorough research and due diligence, investors can identify undervalued REITs that are poised for growth. This approach aligns well with value investing principles, allowing savvy investors to capitalize on market inefficiencies in the real estate sector while enjoying the benefits of income generation through dividends.

Evaluating Technology-Related REITs

Evaluating technology-related Real Estate Investment Trusts (REITs) requires a comprehensive understanding of both the technology sector and real estate dynamics. As technology continues to permeate every aspect of life, certain real estate segments, such as data centers, cell towers, and logistics facilities, have emerged as critical components of a technology-driven economy. Investors should look for REITs that focus on properties providing essential services to tech companies, as these have a unique advantage in an increasingly digital world. A thorough analysis of the underlying assets, their locations, and occupancy rates can reveal potential growth opportunities.

When examining technology-related REITs, one of the key metrics to consider is the dividend yield. Many investors are drawn to REITs for their potential for regular income, and technology-focused REITs can be particularly attractive due to their growth prospects linked to the tech industry's expansion. Evaluating the dividend history and growth rate of these REITs can provide insights into their financial health and long-term sustainability. A consistent track record of increasing dividends often indicates robust cash flow management and a solid investment thesis, making these REITs appealing for dividend growth investing.

Another critical factor in evaluating these REITs is their exposure to technology trends. Investors should assess how well the REIT's portfolio aligns with emerging technologies such as cloud computing, e-commerce, and artificial intelligence. REITs that own properties catering to these sectors may benefit significantly from increased demand, driving up both occupancy rates and rental income. Additionally, understanding the macroeconomic factors influencing the technology landscape can help investors gauge future performance, allowing for strategic investment decisions based on sector-specific trends.

Valuation metrics play a crucial role in assessing technology-related REITs. Price-to-earnings ratios, funds from operations (FFO), and net asset value (NAV) are essential tools for investors looking to identify undervalued opportunities. By comparing these metrics to industry benchmarks, investors can determine whether a REIT is trading at a premium or discount, offering insights into potential investment opportunities. Furthermore, understanding the REIT's balance sheet and debt levels can help investors evaluate its financial stability and risk profile, which is especially important in a fluctuating market.

Finally, considering the impact of Environmental, Social, and Governance (ESG) factors can enhance the evaluation process. Investors increasingly prioritize sustainable and socially responsible investments, and technology-related REITs are no exception. REITs that implement green building practices or contribute positively to local communities can attract a broader investor base and potentially provide higher returns. By integrating ESG criteria into their investment analysis, investors can identify technology-related REITs that not only promise financial performance but also align with ethical investment strategies.

Chapter 12: Technology Stocks with High Market Demand

Identifying Trends in Technology Demand

Identifying trends in technology demand is crucial for investors looking to capitalize on high-growth opportunities. The technology sector is not only dynamic but also often serves as a leading indicator for broader market movements. Understanding what drives demand in this space—be it consumer preferences, regulatory changes, or advancements in innovation—can provide valuable insights for making informed investment decisions. Investors should focus on sectors within technology that show consistent growth patterns, such as cloud computing, artificial intelligence, and cybersecurity, while keeping an eye on emerging technologies that could disrupt the market.

One method to identify trends is through extensive market research and analysis of consumer behavior. Trends can often be spotted by examining sales data, user engagement metrics, and market penetration rates of various technology products and services. For instance, the rise in remote work has significantly boosted demand for collaboration tools and cloud storage solutions, making companies in this space prime candidates for investment. Investors should leverage data analytics tools to track these metrics, allowing them to make data-driven decisions that align with current and future technology demands.

Another important factor to consider is the influence of regulatory changes on technology demand. Laws and regulations can create new market opportunities or restrict existing ones. For example, the increasing focus on data privacy has heightened demand for cybersecurity solutions, as businesses seek to comply with regulations like GDPR and CCPA. By staying informed about legislative developments, investors can position themselves to take advantage of shifts in technology demand, strategically investing in companies poised to benefit from these changes.

Investors should also consider global trends that may affect technology demand. The rapid digital transformation seen in emerging markets presents unique opportunities for high returns. Countries with increasing internet penetration and mobile device adoption are likely to experience a surge in demand for technology products and services. By diversifying their portfolios to include international stocks, investors can tap into these burgeoning markets, potentially yielding significant profits as technology adoption accelerates worldwide.

Lastly, incorporating ESG (Environmental, Social, and Governance) criteria into investment strategies can align with shifting consumer preferences that prioritize sustainability. Companies that demonstrate a commitment to responsible practices are increasingly attracting investment. Identifying technology firms that lead in ESG initiatives can not only fulfill ethical investment goals but also tap into a growing market segment. As awareness of social and environmental issues continues to rise, these companies are likely to experience higher demand and, consequently, higher market valuations, making them attractive candidates for long-term investment.

Strategies for Investing in High-Demand Stocks

Investing in high-demand stocks requires a multifaceted approach, combining various strategies tailored to market trends, investor goals, and risk tolerance. One effective strategy is Dividend Growth Investing, which focuses on companies that not only pay dividends but also consistently increase them over time. By identifying firms with a strong history of dividend growth, investors can benefit from both capital appreciation and a reliable income stream. This strategy is particularly appealing in volatile markets where steady cash flow can mitigate losses and provide a cushion during downturns.

Value Investing in Undervalued Stocks is another robust strategy that can yield significant returns. Investors should look for stocks trading below their intrinsic value, often identified through fundamental analysis. Metrics such as price-to-earnings ratios, price-to-book ratios, and cash flow analysis can help pinpoint these opportunities. By investing in undervalued companies with solid fundamentals, investors position themselves for substantial gains when the market corrects its pricing errors. Patience is key, as realizing the potential of these stocks may take time.

Growth Stocks with High Potential offer another avenue for investors seeking high returns. These stocks typically belong to companies that are expected to grow at an above-average rate compared to their industry peers. Identifying sectors poised for growth, such as technology or renewable energy, can enhance the chances of selecting winning stocks. Investors should conduct thorough research, focusing on innovation, market demand, and competitive advantages. While investing in growth stocks can lead to significant gains, it also comes with higher risks, making it essential to evaluate the overall market conditions and individual company performance.

Sector-Specific Investment Strategies can also be beneficial in navigating high-demand stocks. By concentrating on particular sectors that show promising growth trends, such as artificial intelligence or cybersecurity, investors can capitalize on industry-specific dynamics. Monitoring economic indicators, policy changes, and technological advancements within these sectors can provide insights into future performance. This strategy allows investors to become more knowledgeable about specific industries and make informed decisions that leverage market opportunities.

Options Trading for Income Generation is a sophisticated strategy that can enhance returns while managing risk. Investors can use options to create income through various strategies, such as covered calls or cash-secured puts. By writing options against their existing stock positions, investors can earn premiums while potentially retaining their shares for long-term growth. This approach requires a solid understanding of options mechanics and market conditions. Additionally, diversifying into International Stocks with High Returns or ESG Investing for Sustainable Profits can provide further avenues for growth while aligning investments with personal values and market demands. Each of these strategies offers unique opportunities and risks, underscoring the importance of a well-rounded investment approach.

Chapter 13: Conclusion and Future Outlook

Recap of Key Strategies

In the rapidly evolving landscape of technology investing, understanding and implementing key strategies is crucial for maximizing returns. This subchapter revisits the essential approaches discussed throughout the book, emphasizing their relevance to both novice and seasoned investors. By focusing on high-demand technology stocks, investors can identify the most promising opportunities, balancing risk with potential reward. A comprehensive grasp of these strategies equips investors to navigate the complexities of the tech sector effectively.

Dividend Growth Investing remains a cornerstone strategy for those seeking steady income alongside capital appreciation. This approach involves selecting stocks that not only pay dividends but also have a history of consistently increasing those payments. By focusing on technology companies that prioritize shareholder returns through dividends, investors can benefit from both regular income and the compounding effect of reinvested dividends, making it a reliable choice in a volatile market.

Value Investing in Undervalued Stocks is another critical strategy highlighted in this book. This method involves identifying technology stocks that are trading below their intrinsic value, often due to market misperceptions or short-term challenges. By conducting thorough analyses of financial statements and market conditions, investors can capitalize on these opportunities, purchasing shares at a discount. The key lies in patience and diligent research, as the market may take time to recognize the true value of these stocks.

For those interested in rapid growth potential, focusing on Growth Stocks with High Potential is paramount. These stocks are characterized by above-average earnings growth relative to their industry peers. Investors should look for companies poised for expansion through innovative technologies, market share gains, or new product launches. By identifying and investing in these high-potential growth stocks early, investors can position themselves for significant capital gains as the companies thrive in a competitive market.

Sector-Specific Investment Strategies also play an important role in tech investing. By concentrating on particular sectors such as cybersecurity, artificial intelligence, or cloud computing, investors can harness the momentum of industries that are experiencing explosive growth. Additionally, options trading for income generation and the pursuit of international stocks with high returns further diversify an investor's portfolio. As sustainability becomes increasingly important, ESG Investing for Sustainable Profits offers a way to align investment goals with ethical considerations, ensuring that capital is allocated to companies committed to responsible practices. Lastly, Small-Cap Stocks with Big Potential and Income-Focused REIT Investments provide unique opportunities for investors seeking both growth and income, rounding out a well-structured approach to tech stock investing.

Future Trends in Technology Investing

As the technology landscape continues to evolve at a rapid pace, investors must remain vigilant in identifying future trends that can impact their portfolios. One significant trend is the rise of artificial intelligence (AI) and machine learning. Companies leveraging these technologies are poised for substantial growth, as they enhance operational efficiencies and create innovative products. Investors should monitor firms integrating AI into their business models, as these organizations often exhibit high potential for both growth and profitability, making them prime candidates for investment.

Another trend gaining momentum is the increasing focus on sustainability and Environmental, Social, and Governance (ESG) factors. Investors are becoming more discerning, seeking out companies that prioritize sustainable practices alongside profitability. This shift presents opportunities in sectors such as clean energy, electric vehicles, and sustainable agriculture. Companies that can demonstrate a commitment to ESG principles may not only appeal to socially-conscious investors but also benefit from regulatory incentives and consumer preferences, leading to potentially higher returns.

The expansion of the Internet of Things (IoT) also represents a critical trend in technology investing. As more devices become interconnected, the demand for solutions that can manage, secure, and analyze data will soar. Investors should look for opportunities within companies that specialize in IoT infrastructure, cybersecurity, and big data analytics. These sectors are likely to experience robust growth, providing a fertile ground for both value and growth investors seeking high-potential stocks.

Furthermore, the ongoing digital transformation across various industries continues to create investment opportunities. Companies that facilitate this transition—such as cloud computing providers, cybersecurity firms, and automation technologies—are positioned to benefit significantly. Investors should consider diversifying their portfolios by including sector-specific investment strategies that target these transformative sectors. This approach can mitigate risks while maximizing exposure to high-demand technology stocks.

Lastly, the globalization of technology markets opens doors for international investment strategies. Emerging markets are becoming increasingly important players in the tech industry, offering unique opportunities for growth. Investors should consider diversifying into international stocks with high returns potential, particularly in regions where technology adoption is accelerating. By remaining informed about global trends and leveraging the advantages of international investments, investors can enhance their portfolios and capitalize on the dynamic nature of the technology sector.

www.ingramcontent.com/pod-product-compliance
Lightning Source LLC
Chambersburg PA
CBHW070951220526
45471CB00007B/2983